BOOK ANALYSIS

By Corinne Herward

Trainspotting

BY IRVINE WELSH

IRVINE WELSH

SCOTTISH NOVELIST

- **Born in Leith (Scotland) in 1958.**
- **Notable works:**
  - *The Acid House* (1994), short story collection
  - *Porno* (2002), novel
  - *Skagboys* (2012), novel

Irvine Welsh was born in Leith, the portside area of Edinburgh, in 1958. When Welsh was four his family were granted social housing and they moved to Muirhouse. Welsh left school at 16 and worked as an electrician until he sustained an injury and decided to leave the trade. He moved to London in 1978 and became active in the counter-cultural punk scene. In the 1980s Welsh returned to Edinburgh to work for the social housing department, before studying for his MBA at Herriot-Watt University.

After Welsh returned to Edinburgh, he found some old diaries and drafted what would become his best-known novel, *Trainspotting*. The book follows a small group of friends and the ties that bind them, from their heroin addictions to their social upbringings, their lives in council flats and the AIDS epidemic. In 1993 Secker and Warburg decided to publish the novel, despite believing it would be a commercial failure. The brutality of the book offended many critics, and *Trainspotting* was rejected for the Booker Prize shortlist. Despite this, *Trainspotting* propelled Welsh to fame and was turned into a movie of the same name, directed by Danny Boyle. Welsh continued to write fiction which retains the same influences as *Trainspotting*, and in the early 2000s he moved into screenwriting.

TRAINSPOTTING

A SOCIAL HISTORY OF SCOTTISH DRUG ADDICTION

- **Genre:** novel
- **Reference edition:** Welsh, I. (1999) *Trainspotting*. London: Vintage Classics.
- **1st edition:** 1993
- **Themes:** working-class society, isolation, drug addiction, freedom, choice

The narration of *Trainspotting* is fragmented, reflecting the broken existence of the characters. The novel opens with a section narrated by Mark (also known and Renton, Rent-boy and Rents). Mark is the primary narrator of *Trainspotting*, although there are sections from Simon's (aka Sick Boy's) point of view, as well as others such as Nina, Mark's cousin. The story charts the ebb and flow of Mark and his friends' heroin addictions, recording their efforts to quit, the death of his friends' baby through neglect, their worsening physical and social conditions and eventually the spread of AIDS through the city. Renton attempts to leave Edinburgh for London to shed his friends' co-dependent drug habit but realises that he is in too deep when he gets involved in a drug sale. In a last-ditch effort to free himself of their influence, Mark steals from his friends, including the psychopathic Francis Begbie, and leaves to create a new life in Amsterdam. Whether Mark or anyone else in *Trainspotting* will ever be truly free of heroin is a question that Welsh leaves the reader to decide.

SUMMARY

SPIRALLING ADDICTION

Mark is watching a movie with Sick Boy, who feels symptoms of withdrawal, and insists that they go to visit Johnny Swan, the local dealer, and an addict himself. "Nae friends in this game," Mark remembers Johnny telling him. "Jist associates" (p. 6). Mark shoots up and is carried away on a tide of pleasure. To Mark the heroin is like a beautiful sea, but he also knows the damage it causes: "More short-term sea, more long-term poison" (p. 14). Attempting to quit, Mark barricades himself into an apartment with provisions. However, his effort is short-lived and, unable to find any heroin, Mark settles for opium, sourced from a dealer he despises. When the diarrhoea he suffers removes the opium from his system, Mark dives headfirst into a toilet to retrieve the drug, showing the desperation of the addiction he suffers. When the group are shooting up at Lesley's house, her baby, Dawn, dies. The cause of death is ambiguous, but it is implied that she was neglected while the group were taking drugs. Sick Boy cries, and as Mark looks at him, he realises that he was Dawn's father. The group try to ignore Dawn's death by injecting more heroin. Referencing the chapter title 'It Goes Without Saying', Mark takes the first shot despite Lesley's distress, showing how ingrained their addiction is. Mark's mother shows up at his door and cries through the keyhole, but Mark does not answer, claiming that he loves her so much he wishes she had another son, because he does not think he can change. In 'The Glass', we are introduced to Mark's friend Begbie, who incites a violent pub brawl. Mark knows that Begbie is a psychopath but feels bound to him through friendship. The narration shifts to Tommy. When he goes to an Iggy Pop concert on his girlfriend's birthday, she breaks up with him, and Tommy turns to Mark for heroin, which he supplies, only dimly conscious of the addiction that he is beginning. In 'The First Shag in Ages', Mark briefly gives up heroin. He has sex with a 14-year-old, though he is unaware of her age at first, and despite his fright when he discovers that she is a schoolgirl, he has sex with her again. When walking through a park Mark tries to kill some squirrels, but Spud stops him, comparing their innocence to Dawn's. Mark apologises to Spud, and the pair hug, forgiving each other.

RELAPSE

Mark and Spud go to court for stealing books. The judge suspends Mark's sentence because of his efforts to quit heroin, while Spud gets a ten-month sentence. Unable to celebrate his escape, Mark leaves the pub where his parents and friends are drinking to go to Johnny Swan's, for "ONE hit, jist ONE FUCKIN hit tae git us ower this long, hard, day" (p. 177). In 'Searching for the Inner Man', Mark confesses the source of his heroin addiction, and his history with ineffective counsellors: "Ah despised masel and the world because ah failed tae face up tae ma ain, and life's, limitations." (p. 185). Mark's depression causes him to look to heroin to fill his inner void. After this diatribe, Mark overdoses and is taken home by his mother and father. In withdrawal he sees visions of Dawn, and she accuses him of killing her. Then Mark attempts to return to normalcy, but the inane tedium of it depresses him. Mark's older brother, Billy, dies and after the funeral Mark has sex with Billy's pregnant girlfriend, Sharon. Mark blames the politicians at Westminster for killing Billy, rather than the working-class Republicans. In 'Bad Blood', Welsh returns to the topic of HIV in Scotland through the eyes of Davy. His girlfriend was raped by a man with HIV, and then gave him the disease. Davy pretends to befriend the man, but while he is on his deathbed Davy tortures him with pictures of his child. Davy tells the man that he raped his son and then murdered him, while in truth he merely drugged the child and took pictures. Davy then smothers him, and with his revenge complete he finally begins to process and accept his life with HIV. Alison and Kelly get into a fight with construction workers, and Kelly wonders why men are only decent when they are in the minority. In the next chapter, Mark joins in the bullying that occurs when Kelly gets a fake phone call at work, asking for a 'Mark Hunt' (which sounds like 'my cunt' in a Scottish accent). Mark looks around and realises how unpleasant the laughter is while tears well up in Kelly's eyes.

DISEASE AND DEATH

Matty dies of toxoplasmosis, which he contracts from a kitten he adopted and then mistreated, never cleaning up after it and allowing its faeces to lie around the house. Matty never knew he had HIV, but Gav tells Mark that it created an abscess in his brain. At the funeral Alison vows to keep clean, and Mark agrees, saying "Wir aw gaunnae be wiped oot if we dinnae git it thegither" (p. 291). Mark avoids drugs when he is in London, finding a new boredom in the drugs scene he is so accustomed to. Back in Edinburgh, Kelly is working in the pub while studying for her degree. When upper- to middle-class English men come into the pub and harass her, she mixes their food with her tampons, urinates in their wine and finally serves excrement with their profiteroles. As a result of this incident, Kelly decides that morality is relative. Mark returns to Leith at Christmas and meets Francis Begbie, his psychopathic school friend. He tells Mark that Tommy has HIV and that he should visit him. Mark and Begbie walk up to the train station and meet Begbie's father, an alcoholic. Begbie assaults the next man they meet, leaving him prostrate.

Mark goes to visit Johnny Swan, whose leg has been amputated. Johnny is in good spirits, but when Mark refuses to give in to his nostalgia he becomes bitter. Later Johnny turns to begging, pretending to be an ex-soldier, gloating about the profit and the methadone he receives from the NHS. Meanwhile, Mark goes to visit Tommy in the council flat he is forced to live in. Tommy is surrounded by insults spray-painted on his door, such as "PLAGUER" and "JUNKY" (p. 315). Tommy resents Mark for getting him hooked on heroin and still being clean. Feeling guilty, Mark gives Tommy money. Begbie, Sick Boy, Mark and Spud become involved in a small heroin deal, and on their way to London Mark starts using again to control his nerves. However, when they make the deal in London, Mark double crosses his friends and steals the money. Mark books a ferry to Amsterdam, hoping to start a new life away from Leith, but it is unclear if he will ever truly escape heroin.

CHARACTER STUDY

MARK/RENTON

The protagonist of *Trainspotting* is a cynical character. Mark has a dark outlook on normal life, reflected in his monologue on the monotony of the average life, where he claims: "Well I choose not tae choose life" (p. 187). Heroin has replaced other forms of intimacy for Mark, and unable to find any romantic fulfilment due to his heroin use, he also gradually becomes estranged from his friends, believing that they are all just associates in pursuit of another kick. Mark's family add to his isolation, from his mentally incapacitated brother, his father and older brother's Unionist politics and his parents' love of reality television and bingo. Mark ultimately attempts to break with heroin by betraying his friends and leaving Leith behind.

SIMON/SICK BOY

Sick Boy is a cold and callous womaniser who often sees himself as a James Bond character. With his good looks and charm, Sick Boy is a natural con artist and often steals from the women he sleeps with. Sick Boy is also Dawn's father, and though he denies responsibility at the time, it is implied that he feels guilty about her death. Sick Boy effortlessly moves through life and manipulates Mark's parents to see him as a shining example to their son, a man who would never touch drugs outside of a youthful experimentation. A slippery, seemingly untouchable and immoral pimp, Sick Boy is a representation of what Mark could be if he did not have a conscience.

DANNY/SPUD

The innocent soul of *Trainspotting*, Spud is depicted as a well-meaning and good-hearted, if not very clever person, who is the last remnant of goodness in the middle of Mark's heroin addiction. It is Spud who asks his friends to stand by Lesley and flush the heroin down the toilet when Dawn dies, and it is Spud who stops Mark from murdering the squirrels in the park. However, he seems ill-equipped to participate in normal life. Unable to lie his way slickly through a job interview with the ease the Mark shows, he is honest, and as a result is rejected. Spud is also the one to be imprisoned for ten months after a theft, despite Mark's involvement. He is the only person that Mark feels bad about betraying at the end of the novel.

BEGBIE

Francis Begbie is a psychopath, who represents the unbreakable ties that Mark has to Leith. Mark describes how in every school setting he was placed next to Franco (as he is nicknamed), until he worked his way up the academic stream, and Begbie was taken away to a juvenile detention centre. Begbie is not a heroin addict, and although he drinks heavily his true addiction seems to be to violence and holding power over others. Begbie claims to protect his friends, but Mark knows that Begbie's real friends are other violent psychopaths. In 'Strolling Through the Meadows', Spud claims that Begbie "rapes" the men, "sort ay shafted us up oor erses n peyed us oaf," when he forces them to carry out his violent attacks (p. 155). Mark admits that he pacifies Begbie in order not to become another victim. Mark uses Begbie's violent nature to distance himself from Leith, from heroin and from his history.

TOMMY

Tommy is the most clean-cut of Mark's friends. In the first half of the novel, Tommy represents someone who 'chooses life.' He is a football fan and a music lover, with a beautiful girlfriend who provokes envy in the other men. However, when Tommy prioritises an Iggy Pop concert over his relationship, his girlfriend, Liz, breaks up with him. Tommy takes heroin from Mark to shake the depression from his breakup, and his predisposition to the drug triggers an almost immediate addiction. Tommy's life weighs on Mark's mind in later chapters when he learns that Tommy has caught HIV from infected needles. "Tommy will not survive winter in West Granton," Mark remarks from a position of privilege, visiting the situation that he was once in (p. 317). Mark gives Tommy money, but he cannot give him the heroin that he craves, as Mark has shaken his addiction by the time that Tommy is dying.

ANALYSIS

CHOICE

In *Trainspotting*'s best-known diatribe, Renton justifies his heroin addiction by pointing out the meaninglessness of the lives that ordinary people carve out for themselves. "Choose life," Renton says, quoting the well-known anti-drug campaign:

> "Choose mortgage payments; choose washing machines; choose cars; choose sitting oan a couch watching mind-numbing and spirit-crushing game shows, stuffing fucking junk food intae yir mooth. Choose rotting away, pishing and shiteing yersel in a home, a total fuckin embarrassment tae the selfish, fucked-up brats ye've produced. Choose life." (p. 187)

However, Renton's choice to continue his heroin-fuelled existence is not a choice at all, but an addiction. Spud recognises this when he stops Mark from killing some squirrels in the park: "Ah hate it the way Mark's intae hurtin animals... Ye cannae love yirsel if ye want tae hurt things like that... He's free. That's mibbe what Rents cannae stand." (p. 159). In 'The First Day of the Edinburgh Festival', Mark attempts to quit, renting an isolated flat and stockpiling tins of soup to stop him from going outside. However, his resolution is short-lived, and he attempts to get hold of a dealer for what Mark tells himself is his final shot, a last goodbye. "Two choices," Mark considers, "one: tough it oot, back in the room, two: phone that cunt Forrester and go tae Muirhouse, get fucked aboot and ripped oaf wi some crap gear. Nae contest" (p. 16). The lack of agency and independent action is also a problem that Mark experiences with his social life. Although he is dissatisfied with his toxic friends, Mark feels that they are tied together by history, and he struggles to see their connections as something that can be severed. "He really is a cunt ay the first order," Mark says of Begbie. "The big problem is, he's a mate n aw. Whit kin ye dae?" (p. 84). Mark cites the seating charts in primary school as a basis for his unquestioning loyalty to the violent, psychopathic Begbie. This is one of the reasons that the conclusion of *Trainspotting* can be read as a positive and optimistic outcome. Mark chooses to abandon his friends, knowing that he is betraying them and leaving them forever, choosing to put himself first in order to find a better life. If Mark regresses into heroin addiction it will be his own decision and not due to the influence of his friends or his environment.

COMMUNITY

The fragmented structure of *Trainspotting* indicates the isolation that is experienced by the characters. Each story is a segmented chapter told from the point of view of one of the characters. The stream of consciousness technique that Welsh employs roots the reader in the characters' minds, allowing us to experience their loneliness, selfishness and desperation. The destruction of community is a topic that Welsh introduces in the first chapter of *Trainspotting*, 'The Skag Boys.' In it, Mark reflects on the state of friendship with Sick Boy and Johnny Swan. Mark does not want to help Sick Boy, as he would rather stay home and watch videos: "Ah'm really fuckin sufferin here, n ma so-called mate's draggin his feet deliberately, lovin every fuckin minute ay it!" (p. 4). Mark cares more about the 50 cents that he has spent on a video than about helping Sick Boy. Johnny Swan enjoys the same egotistical self-centredness. Mark talks about how Johnny Swan was once a friend of his that he played football with. Swanny warned him that there were no friends in a junkie's life, only associates: "Ah thought he was bein harsh, flippant and show-oafy, until ah got sae far in. Now ah ken precisely what the cunt meant" (p. 6). Johnny Swan enjoys the power he holds over the two men while they wait for their shots and taunts them: "'Ye git a shot, but only if ye use this gear. Wir playin trust games theday,' he smiled but he wisnae jokin" (p. 9). Mark cannot believe that this is the kind-hearted football enthusiast that he grew up with, a gentle joker, someone who would wash everyone's football kit and never complain: "Some malicious demon had invaded his body and poisoned his mind" (*ibid.*). It becomes clear as the book goes on that this poison is heroin, and that it drives the characters apart. Mark praises heroin for its ability to streamline the necessities of life, as a junkie only cares about how to get his next hit. However, it is obvious that this quality erases the need and the appreciation for social circles. In 'It Goes Without Saying', Spud says that he is cooking up, and Mark wonders if he has spoken at all in the last few days except to say this. "Obviously the cunt's spoken ower this period," Mark says defensively. "He must huv, surely tae fuck" (p. 52). Similarly, Spud's plea for the men to stand by Lesley after Dawn's death highlights the cynical and empty existence of a heroin user. At the threat of having to flush their gear down the toilet, Mark, Sick Boy and Matty refuse to call the police after Dawn's death. "That sort ay solidarity seems a bit ay a fanciful notion in the circumstances," Mark says of Spud's suggestion (p. 53). To Mark, friendship is merely a side-effect of existing under the same conditions. Mark extends the same apathy to his family, never offering any comfort to his parents after the death of their other sons, and merely being depressed by their activities. Welsh offers no redemption for the torn-apart structure of Scottish society, suggesting that heroin is an encompassing addiction that takes over an addict's life.

EMPIRICISM

Scottish culture has been shaped by the relationship between Scotland and England, which historically has been detrimental to Scotland. Economically disadvantaged and controlled by

England, Scottish identity has been fractured, and this tension is explored throughout *Trainspotting*. "Ah despised masel because ah failed to face up tae ma own, and life's limitations," Mark says to explain his drug abuse (p. 185). The limitations of life spent in Scotland are a theme which crops up repeatedly as Welsh traces the working-class life carved out by heroin addicts. "Scotland is one of the most repressed societies," Welsh claimed in a 1996 interview (Berman, 1996: 60). The self-hatred that the dispossessed Scottish men feel is internalised and results in anti-social behaviour, directed at minorities, as well as self-harm. The inability of working-class Scottish men to merge with society is epitomised by Spud and his disastrous interview. When the interviewer asks Spud about his school record, Spud admits that he attended a less prestigious school, St Augustine's. "Ah jist pit doon Heriot's because ah thoat it wid likes, help us git the joab. Too much discrimination in this town, man, ken, likesay?" Spud explains (p. 65). "I was just making conversation, as I did happen to attend Heriot's," the interviewer answers coldly (p. 66). Spud, despite his enthusiasm, does not receive a job offer. Mark, however, who has little interest in the available job, easily charms the interviewer by his ability to convince him that he too is a private school boy, a well-brought-up young man, fallen on hard times. The ability to switch between Scots dialect and British received pronunciation is a privilege that not all are able to access, Welsh suggests, an ability which allows people to merge into the mainstream space, and as a result, to prosper. Spud's inability to merge into a professional space shows his economic and social marginalisation, while the overriding theme of addiction shows the alienation of the blue-collar worker, and their failure to find a space in society. Despite the national marginalisation experienced by the characters, they lash out at those around them, including immigrants. In 'Victory on New Year's Day', the Hearts football fans turn from abusing a male Celtic supporter to heckling an Asian woman and her two small children. "Fuckin Paki slag!'" the fans jeer, "Fuck off back tae yir ain country" (p. 49). Ironically, many critics believe that the success of Trainspotting is empirical in its own right. "The promotion of a particular minority voice as representative of a whole nation's struggle for emancipatory self-expression must inevitably occur at the expense of all other subordinate and disempowered groups," Innes claims. (Innes, 2007: 301). In other words, Innes claims that the immense popularity enjoyed by *Trainspotting* has drowned out smaller Scottish authors, creating a homogenous view of Scottish society. Regardless, when *Trainspotting* emerged in 1993, it did so by giving a voice to people who had been voiceless and by wording the struggle of a working-class Scottish man questioning what it means to "choose life."

FURTHER REFLECTION

SOME QUESTIONS TO THINK ABOUT...

- Why do you think baby Dawn's death is ambiguous? In your own words, suggest a reason that Welsh might make her cause of death unclear.
- The isolation experienced by heroin addicts is dwelt on repeatedly by *Trainspotting*'s main narrator, Mark Renton. By the conclusion of the novel, does Mark have anyone that he does not consider a mere associate?
- Nationalism is at the forefront of the politics of *Trainspotting*, and Mark simultaneously loathes the British as well as the Scottish. Why do some of the characters, such as Tommy, care so much about Scotland, while others hate even that?
- Many of the characters in *Trainspotting* identify strongly with pop culture. Tommy sacrifices his relationship to go to an Iggy Pop concert, while Simon often imagines himself as James Bond. What do these identities represent to characters such as Tommy and Simon?

- *Trainspotting* is often praised for its ability to alleviate the grim lives of the characters with black humour. Write a short paragraph about one moment from the book that made you laugh.
- The conclusion of the novel is unclear. Mark leaves his friends, their toxic habits and Leith behind him. However, he flees to Amsterdam, the European capital of legalised drugs and prostitution, the two reasons that Mark lost his student grant. In your opinion, is the ending hopeful or unhopeful?
- In *The Acid House,* (1994) a later book by Irvine Welsh, he states, "The Scottish Hardman ladders his tights, so he rips open the face of a passer-by... chips a nail so he headbutts some poor fucker." (Welsh, 1994: 276). Why is the gendered violence experienced by Kelly and June so common in the world of *Trainspotting*?
- The title of *Trainspotting* comes from one of the smaller and lesser-known stories of the book. Why do you think Welsh chose this title?

We want to hear from you!
Leave a comment on your online library
and share your favourite books on social media!

FURTHER READING

REFERENCE EDITION

- Welsh, I. (1999) *Trainspotting*. London: Vintage Classics.

REFERENCE STUDIES

- Berman, J. (1996) Irvine Welsh in *BOMB*. [Online]. [Accessed 24 February 2019]. Available from: <https://bombmagazine.org/articles/irvine-welsh/>

- Innes, K. (2007) Mark Renton's Bairns: Identity and Language in the Post-*Trainspotting* Novel. In: B. Schoene ed., *The Edinburgh Companion to Contemporary Scottish Literature.* Edinburgh: Edinburgh University Press, pp. 300-325.

- Welsh, I. (2008) *The Acid House*. London: Random House.

ADDITIONAL SOURCES

- Jones, C. (2010) Welsh and Gender. In: B. Schoene ed., *The Edinburgh Companion to Irvine Welsh*. Edinburgh: Edinburgh University Press pp 45-65.

- Senekal, B.A. (2010) Alienation in Irvine Welsh's *Trainspotting*. *Literator*. [Online]. [Accessed 24 February 2019]. Available from: <https://literator.org.za/index.php/literator/article/view/35olume>

ADAPTATIONS

- *Trainspotting.* (1996) [Film]. Danny Boyle. Dir. England: Channel 4 Films.

www.brightsummaries.com

Ebook EAN: 9782808018913

Paperback EAN: 9782808018920

Legal Deposit: D/2019/12603/112

Cover: © Primento

Digital conception by Primento, the digital partner of
publishers.